A Kaleidoscope Of Poems

Myriad of thoughts coming to life

Anoushka Augustine

BookLeaf Publishing

India | USA | UK

Made with ❤ on the BookLeaf Publishing Platform
www.bookleafpub.in
www.bookleafpub.com

Dedication

This book is dedicated to all those who believe in the transformative journey our lives take us on. As you turn the pages to read, may the poems resonate the infinite emotions and thoughts we all carry within, and remind you that you are special.

Preface

Kaleidoscope of Poems - Is a collection of the experiences that we encounter everyday teaching us to walk through life with heads held high.
The poems reflect our shared experiences which make us question our purpose and who we are!

Acknowledgements

Thank you to my family, friends and my mentors who have given me the impetus to reach the moon and stars and making my dreams come true.

I. LIFE AS WE KNOW IT

Life, a four-letter word so true,

Days surround us in silence, profound and deep,

In moments awake, the dreams we keep.

Look beyond to the kaleidoscope deep,

Guiding us along the treacherous way.

Life, with its mountains steep,

Each hue a step, with lows and highs,

We chase the dreams that we must seek.

In this vast journey, yours and mine.

The road is long, the paths unknown,

Yet in the light, we find a life of our own.

II. THE CREVICES OF HAPPINESS

When the heart gets a blow
When the steps become slow,
When the mind knows it's time,
I close my eyes and wait for the day.
When my life will ever be the same again,
When I will be happy again,
The sun will rise with hope anew,
And skies will shine in brighter blue.
When laughter fills the air I breathe,
I'll find the peace I've longed to see,
For happiness will come to me!
For happiness will come to me!.

III. BETWEEN THE CHAPTERS

Each year a page, each day a line,
We write our story, so pure and divine,
The chapters turn, the milestones age like fine wine,
In every tear, in every sigh.
Through battles fought, through seeds we sow.
With every turn, the lessons show,
The strength within, the will to glow.
We search for moments, bold and bright,
For love to find, for dreams to ignite.
To be seen, to be heard, to take flight,
A purpose to carry, a spark in the night.
But time is fleeting, and one day we'll see,
The chapters close, and we'll be free.
Our names may fade, like whispers in wind,
But stars in the galaxy, we'll always shine.
We are the stars, scattered far and wide,
Each one a memory, to beam with pride,
And in the end, when the chapters close
We'll be the light that will forever glow.

IV. LOST SOULS

Lost souls, dancing through hues of light,
Chasing dreams that are sparkling bright,
With every musical step, they leave behind
A trail of love and joy to find.
Their laughter echoes through the years,
A symphony of joy, beyond the tears,
For in their hearts, they carry all,
The beauty found in life's wondrous souls.
Through sunlit days and starry skies,
They've seen the world with open eyes,
From mountain peaks to oceans wide,
Their spirits soar, their hearts collide.
Memories bloom like flowers sweet,
In every moment, they find their beat,
With every sunset, every dawn,
A story of life, forever drawn.
For lost they may be, yet found they are,
In every laugh, in every star,
Lost souls discovering endless joy.

V. A DANCE OF HEARTS

Hearts collide with gentle gaze,
A dance of love in perfect ways.
The moment's magic, pure and bright,
A spark of love, that shines like light.

Soft whispers, tender touch ignite,
Hearts beating through the night.
The rhythm of love, a symphony sweet,
A dance of hearts, that skip a beat.

In the silence, eyes speak loudly,
A language of love, a heartfelt song,
The unspoken words, a love so true,
A connection deep, between me and you.

Together they sway, a perfect beat,
A love dance, where two hearts meet.
With every step, a love so strong,
A bond of hearts, that will last forevermore.

VI. CELESTIAL HARMONY

We are the cosmic dance, of sun and moon's sweet sway,
A harmony of opposites, in celestial array.
The stars up high, a twinkling sea,
Reflecting the sparkling shine.

Like galaxies colliding, our souls entwine,
In a cosmic waltz, of love and divine,
The sun's warm rays, ignite our inner light,
Guiding us forward, through the dark of night.

We are the universe, unfolding its design,
A majestic symphony, of love and cosmic rhyme.
We shine like stardust, with a light so bold,
Connected, united, under the celestial sun to hold.

VII. TIMELESS

Since time immemorial everything seemed vague,
Time slipped out of my hands with every breath I take,
As years flew past me, shadows of myself kept me
awake.

Everything I do, every step I take makes me want to take
a break.
In yesterday's haze , I searched for a glimpse of me,
A fleeting moment's peace, from the chaos that I could
see,

So let the shadows dance, upon the walls of my mind,
For in their silhouettes, I'll find the pieces of my past left
behind,
And though time may be timeless, its memories forever
mine,
I'll hold on to the moments, that will keep me grounded
and fine.

VIII. A TAPESTRY OF TALES

One world, endless stories spun,
Each thread a journey, each tale begun.
Woven with emotions all singing in unison.
Every story waiting to be read,
Whispers of dreams that must be said.
In quiet corners, voices wait,
To share their truths, to open gates.
The untold stories, veiled in time,
Like hidden treasures, steeped in time,
From every soul, a tale untold,
Some speak of love that knows no end.
Others of hearts that still mend.
Each story carries a different sound,
Yet all are equal, deeply profound.
One world, numerous stories bright,
Together they blaze in endless light.
One world ,where tapestry of tales forever pour.

IX. NATURE'S SMILE

Through nature's smile,
The sun softly weaves,
Golden rays that dance on streams,
Whispers of joy through the trees.
Breezes hum a gentle tune,
Underneath the silver moon,
Stars like diamonds softly gleam,
Reflecting dreams, a tranquil beam.
Mountains stand with immense grace,
In nature's arms, a warm embrace.
The earth, in silence, softly smiles
As day to night slowly flies.

X. COMFORT ZONE

We love to be in our shell,
Our comfort zone where all is well.
It keeps us warm and tight,
Where our dreams take gentle flight.
The world outside is loud and wide,
But in our shell we are safe and beaming with pride.
Yet, a whisper calls from deep inside,
A voice that asks, "What if you tried?"
What if the world could be your friend,
If you let go and learned to bend?
The shell, so warm, is all we've known,
But outside, there's a world of unknown.
The comfort zone, it has its charms,
But growth begins when we take arms.
To step outside and brave the storm,
And find new ways to keep us warm.

XI. EMBERS OF THE PHOENIX

Rising from the ashes,

We ignite our souls,

Above and beyond the never-ending sails.

Embers of the phoenix,

Burning bright,

In the dark of night,

We take flight,

Forever reborn in eternal light.

XII. THE TWO PATHS

Standing gauging the two paths in front of me,
I judge which path will align with my life's destiny.
One path is worn and familiar, a well-trodden way,
The other, uncertain and new, beckons me to seize the
day.

My heart is torn between the two, as I weigh the pros
and cons,
Fear and doubt come creeping, like shadows that linger
on.
But then I think of the days, I've played it safe and
sound,
And how the greatest rewards, often lie just beyond the
ground.

So, I take a deep breath, and choose the path less known,
For in the end, it's not the path, that defines who I'll be,
But the courage to take the leap, and follow my heart's
decree.

XIII. CONSTELLATION OF STARS

Stars brightening up the sky,
Twinkling through the shadow of the moon,
Glimpses of constellations, humans intertwined,
Reflecting our shared journeys, all too soon.
Each star a story, a life once known,
A constellation of souls, together grown.
Echoing moments where hearts intertwine.
Our experiences reflected in each light,
A universe of souls, burning bright,
Together we rise, we fall, we learn,
Like constellations, forever we return.

XIV. SEASONS

Seasons come and go, like the rhythm of life,
In spring, my leaves will bloom again, a fresh start,
Summer keeps me in its warmth, nurturing my growth,
The monsoon arrives, washing away sorrows,
Autumn sheds the leaves, releasing the past,
And in winter, I rest, finding peace in stillness.
Each season is a new chapter, a time of transformation,
Spring plants seeds of hope, while summer brings them to life,
The monsoon cleanses and heals, washing away the old,
Autumn teaches me to release, to let go with grace,
Winter holds me still, a pause before renewal begins.
Time passes in the dance of nature,
Where each season brings its own story,
Ever-changing, ever-evolving,
And life moves forward with every cycle.

XV. LIKE KITES IN THE SKY

Kites in the sky, they soar so high,
While I sit below, gazing at the sky.
I recall the moments, bright sunlit days,
When I flew, feeling free in the wind's gentle praise.

But then came the storm, with a fierce, wild blow,
And those cherished memories scattered below.
Kites are always better when they fly unified.

In the quiet, I long for the days when I too,
Soared with others, the skies a vibrant hue.
But now all that's left is the wind's cold sigh,
As I watch the kites fade, flying far far away from me .

XVI. THE SILENT LOVERS

Lovers, the silent ones, they find,
Confessing love is hard to bind,
Yet still, they don't shy from the test,
They show their love through actions best.
With eyes that speak what words can't say,
Their gaze alone can light the way.
A smile that holds the truth so pure,
A warmth that makes the heart endure.
In every gesture, every touch,
They weave a tale that says so much.
Their love, unspoken, still it sings,
A language that the heartstrings bring.

XVII. HOW HARD CAN IT BE!

How hard can it be to believe in yourself,
When doubts like shadows sit on the shelf?
How hard to imagine a life without love,
When all that you cherish seems distant above?
How hard can it be to carry on,
When the ones you hold dear are suddenly gone?
How hard can it be to face the unknown,
When you feel so lost and all alone?
But it's not hard when you start to see,
The strength inside, the power to be free.
To live authentically, true to your core,
Embrace the journey, let your spirit soar.
For the hardest part is letting go of fear,
Trusting yourself, knowing you're near.
For the hardest part is letting fear fade,
Trusting your heart, the choices you've made.

XVIII. INFINTY AND BEYOND

I ponder to myself if there is infinity and beyond,
Where the body dances freely, to the rhythm of the dawn.
Music fills the air, and art paints the sky,
Creativity meets the galaxy, where stars never die.
The Milky Way whispers, constellations in tune,
A universe of wonder, beneath a cosmic moon.
Where every movement and thought is profound,
And the soul finds its home, safe and sound.

XIX. THE LANGUAGE OF DANCE

With every beat, my spirit lifts,
A joyous rhythm, a heart that sifts
Through joy and light, in every move,
The language of dance begins to prove.
Feet that tap, and arms that fly,
A celebration beneath the sky.
The floor becomes my canvas bright,
I paint with every step, day and night.
Laughter echoes, a pure delight,
In dance, I find my inner light.
A fluttering heart, a soaring soul,
In every gesture, I feel whole.
The joy I feel, it can't be told,
It's in my body, free and bold.
With every twist, with every sound,
In dance, my joy is always found.

XX. ACROSS THE GALAXY

I ponder to myself if there is infinity and beyond,
Where the body dances freely, to the rhythm of the dawn.
Music fills the air, and art paints the sky,
Creativity meets the galaxy, where stars never die.
The Milky Way whispers, constellations in tune,
A universe of wonder, beneath a cosmic moon.
Where every movement and thought is profound,
And the soul finds its home, safe and sound.

XXI. A NEW DAWN

In the crevices of life as we know it,
Between the chapters, lost souls roam,
Searching for the rhythm, the dance of hearts,
In a celestial harmony where time is home.

A tapestry of tales woven in the light,
Nature's smile shines through the seasons' flight,
Like kites in the sky, soaring free,
Caught between the pull of what was and what will be.

In the comfort zone, we stand still,
Yet, the embers of the Phoenix ignite our will.
The two paths before us, mysterious and wide,
A constellation of stars, our hearts collide.

How hard can it be, to find our way!
Through the silent lovers of night and day,
Embracing the infinite, we dream and believe,
As we dance across the galaxy, we weave.
For in the language of dance, a new dawn is born.